What Would YOU Do?

The Underground Railroad

Would YOU Help Them Escape?

Elaine Landau

Enslow Elementary

an imprint of

 Enslow Publishers, Inc.

40 Industrial Road
Box 398
Berkeley Heights, NJ 07922
USA

http://www.enslow.com

Enslow Elementary, an imprint of Enslow Publishers, Inc.
Enslow Elementary® is a registered trademark of Enslow Publishers, Inc.

Library of Congress Cataloging-in-Publication Data

Landau, Elaine.
    The underground railroad : would you help them escape? / by Elaine Landau.
        pages cm. — (What would you do?)
    Includes index.
    Summary: "Discover the risks and rewards of the underground railroad. Readers decide what they would do, and then find out
        what really happened"—Provided by publisher.
    ISBN 978-0-7660-4225-4
    1. Underground Railroad—Juvenile literature. 2. Fugitive slaves—United States—History—19th century—Juvenile literature.
        3. Antislavery movements—United States—History—19th century—Juvenile literature. I. Title.
    E450.L3156 2014
    973.7'115—dc23

                                    2013008788

Future editions:
Paperback ISBN: 978-1-4644-0393-4
EPUB ISBN: 978-1-4645-1216-2
Single-User PDF ISBN: 978-1-4646-1216-9
Multi-User PDF ISBN: 978-0-7660-5848-4

Printed in the United States of America

052014 Lake Book Manufacturing, Inc., Melrose Park, IL

10 9 8 7 6 5 4 3 2 1

To Our Readers: We have done our best to make sure all Internet Addresses in this book were active and appropriate when we went to press. However, the author and the publisher have no control over and assume no liability for the material available on those Internet sites or on other Web sites they may link to. Any comments or suggestions can be sent by e-mail to comments@enslow.com or to the address on the back cover.

♻ Enslow Publishers, Inc., is committed to printing our books on recycled paper. The paper in every book contains 10% to 30% post-consumer waste (PCW). The cover board on the outside of each book contains 100% PCW. Our goal is to do our part to help young people and the environment too!

Every effort has been made to locate all copyright holders of material used in this book. If any errors or omissions have occurred, corrections will be made in future editions of this book.

Illustration Credits: ©Clipart.com, p. 12; *Appletons' Cyclopædia of American Biography*, 1900, v. 4, p. 32(top), p. 43(bottom right); Courtesy of the Levi Coffin Association and Waynet, Inc., pp. 24, 43(top left, top middle); Enslow Publishers, Inc., pp. 4, 16, 28; Image from *Scenes in the Life of Harriet Tubman*, 1869, by Sarah H. Bradford, pp. 27, p. 43(bottom, middle); Library of Congress, pp, 6, 7, 8, 11, 23, 31, 32(bottom), 35(both), 36, 39, 40, 43 (top right, bottom left), National Weather Service, Pittsburgh, Pennsylvania, p. 20; ©Thinkstock/Photos.com, pp.1, 15, 19.

Cover Illustration: Library of Congress

Contents

Who Had Slaves?

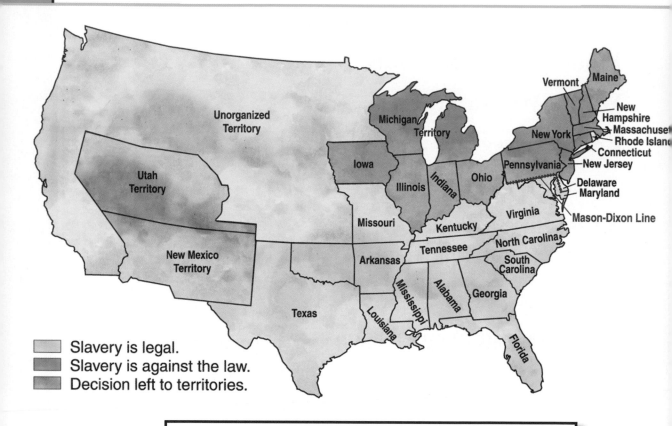

Vermont • Maine • New Hampshire • Massachusetts • Rhode Island • Connecticut • New Jersey • New York • Pennsylvania • Delaware • Maryland • Mason-Dixon Line

Michigan Territory • Iowa • Illinois • Indiana • Ohio • Missouri • Kentucky • Virginia • North Carolina • Tennessee • Arkansas • South Carolina • Mississippi • Alabama • Georgia • Louisiana • Texas • Florida

Unorganized Territory • Utah Territory • New Mexico Territory

Slavery is legal.
Slavery is against the law.
Decision left to territories.

By the early 1800s, slavery was abolished in all states north of the border of Pennsylvania and Maryland. Trouble was growing between the slave owners of the South and the abolitionists of the North.

Land of the Free

The United States of America. Today this country stands for freedom. But that was not always so. From the early 1600s until 1865, slavery was legal in parts of the country.

Most slaves' lives were brutal. Many worked in the fields from sun up to sun down. It was often backbreaking work. Slaves who slowed down might be harshly whipped. Most slaves were poorly fed and clothed. They often lived in broken down shacks. These homes were cold in the winter and hot in the summer.

For many slaves, there was no way out. Escaping alone was difficult and dangerous. Owners hired

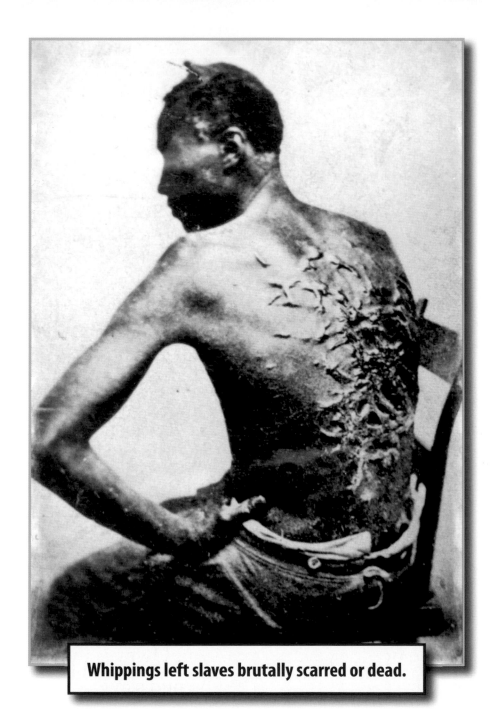

Whippings left slaves brutally scarred or dead.

The neck ring was used as a punishment for running away.

slave catchers to catch them. They used dogs to hunt runaways down. Returned slaves were brutally punished as an example to others. They might be nearly whipped to death or tortured. Sometimes, they were put in uncomfortable chains. They also might be branded with a hot iron. Owners branded them with the letter "R" for returned slave.

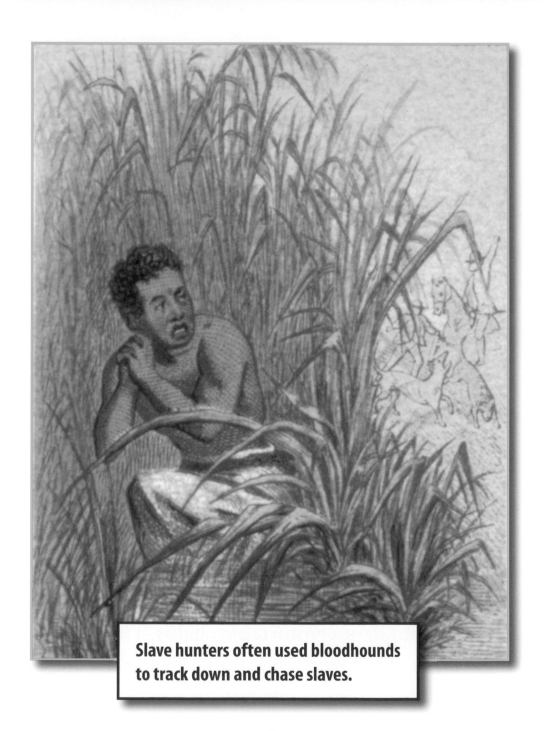

Slave hunters often used bloodhounds to track down and chase slaves.

What Would YOU Do?

What would you do if you were a slave?

❋ Would you try to escape? Would you know where to run? *Or . . .*

❋ Would you stay where you are? Running away without help might be even more deadly than slavery.

Finding Another Choice

Some slaves escaped on their own. They took a chance. In time, more slaves learned about another choice. It was known as the Underground Railroad.

The Underground Railroad was not a real railroad. It wasn't underground either. It was a secret network of people working together. Its goal was to help slaves escape to freedom.

The Underground Railroad was run by people who were against slavery. Some of these people were called Abolitionists. They wanted to outlaw or "abolish" slavery. The people working on the Underground Railroad were willing to break the law to help slaves escape. Often they led slaves out at night. Along the

The arrest and trial of Anthony Burns under the Fugitive Slave Act of 1850 touched off riots and protests by abolitionists and citizens of Boston in 1854. A portrait of the twenty-four-year-old Burns is surrounded by scenes of his life.

way, they'd hide the runaways in their homes and barns. There were even some runaway slaves working with the Underground Railroad. They risked sneaking back into the South to bring others out. They were especially helpful because they knew the area and back roads so well.

Slaveholders hated the Underground Railroad. They did whatever they could to stop it. The Fugitive Slave Act of 1793 made helping slaves escape illegal. Later, the Fugitive Slave Act of 1850 was passed. It strengthened the earlier law. Slaveholders tried to have the Underground Railroad workers arrested and punished. They offered large rewards for their capture.

These people are helping escaping slaves on a stop on the Underground Railroad.

Often Southern courts gave the workers large fines. Most Underground Railroad workers were not rich. A very large fine could put them out of business.

Other times slaveholders took matters into their own hands. They had Underground Railroad workers beat up. They destroyed their property. They tried to force them out of the South.

What Would YOU Do?

✸ **Would you have the courage to work on the Underground Railroad?** *Or . . .*

✸ **Would you pass on working on the Underground Railroad? Would you help the railroad in other ways? Would you give money to their cause? Maybe you would ask your congressman to change the laws that allow slavery.**

What a Way to Travel!

Lots of people helped with the Underground Railroad. They did this in all sorts of ways. Many people were needed. The Underground Railroad was quite a large system. One route took escaping slaves from Virginia and Kentucky across the Ohio River to freedom. Other routes ran from Maryland through Pennsylvania, New York, and the New England states. Slavery was not allowed in Canada. So the Underground Railroad also helped escaping slaves get there.

Terms used on the Underground Railroad were like those used on a real railroad. The stops along the routes were called stations. These were people's

These slaves are escaping from the eastern shore of Maryland at night.

homes, barns, and sheds. They'd hide slaves there during the day. Some of these places had special trap doors built in them. These led to hidden areas for the slaves to hide in. The different stations were owned by Underground Railroad agents. They fed and cared for the slaves while they were at the stations. The Underground Railroad had conductors too. They led the runaways from station to station.

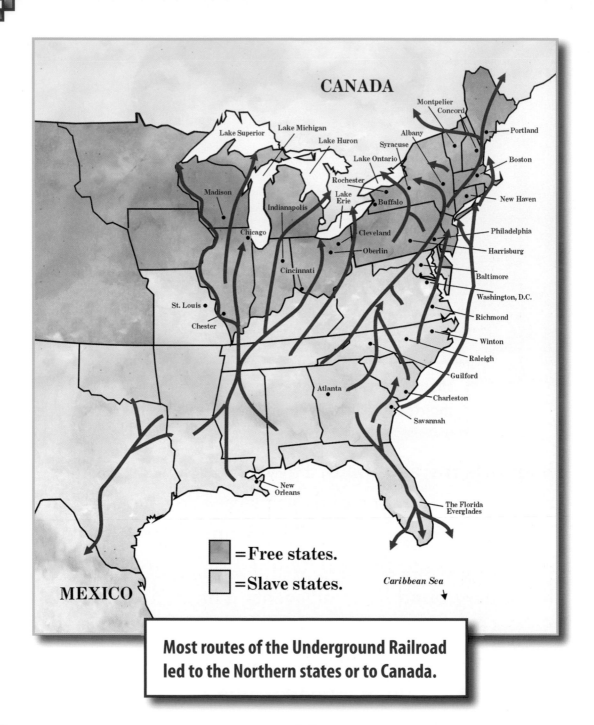

CANADA

Lake Superior • Lake Michigan • Lake Huron • Lake Ontario • Rochester • Lake Erie • Buffalo

Montpelier • Concord • Albany • Syracuse • Portland • Boston • New Haven

Madison • Indianapolis • Chicago • Cleveland • Oberlin

Philadelphia • Harrisburg • Baltimore • Washington, D.C. • Richmond

Cincinnati

St. Louis • Chester

Winton • Raleigh • Guilford

Atlanta • Charleston • Savannah

New Orleans • The Florida Everglades

=Free states.
=Slave states.

Caribbean Sea

MEXICO

Most routes of the Underground Railroad led to the Northern states or to Canada.

What Would YOU Do?

What would you do if you were a slave ready to run?

✿ Would you make a daring move and try to escape on your own? *Or . . .*

✿ Would you wait for a chance to travel with other runaways from station to station on the Underground Railroad?

Bold Bravery

Many slaves made dangerous and bold escapes. Among the most famous escapes was that of Eliza Harris. Eliza Harris was a slave from Kentucky. She had heard some terrible news. She and her child were to be sold off to different masters. Eliza knew she had to escape.

It was a very cold winter that year. Eliza hoped that the Ohio River would be frozen solid. She planned to carry her baby across it. But when she reached the river, the ice had broken into large chunks.

At first, Eliza waited for the ice to harden. Yet Eliza knew that her master had sent slave catchers after her. By now, they had to be very near.

Before long, the slave catchers spotted her. Eliza made a run for it. Tightly clinging to her baby, she

A scene from *Uncle Tom's Cabin* by Harriet Beecher Stowe. The hero of the book is Eliza, a slave woman who escapes to freedom while carrying her baby in her arms. The book is loosely based on the real-life story of Eliza Harris.

Ice in the Ohio River—dangerous to cross both today and in Eliza's time

jumped onto a chunk of floating river ice. From there, she jumped from ice floe to ice floe. She hoped to cross the river that way.

It was not easy. Sometimes the ice floes sunk under the weight of her body. When this happened, she had to quickly get herself and her baby to another chunk of floating ice. They could have died in the icy river but Eliza finally made it across.

A man standing on the other side of the river had been watching. He helped Eliza and her child out of the water. From there, the two were taken to an Underground Railroad station. They kept going North. At last they crossed a lake that took them to freedom in Canada.

What Would YOU Do?

❀ If you were Eliza, would you risk your child's life crossing the icy river? *Or . . .*

❀ Would you have felt that being a slave was better than drowning in a freezing river? Also, you wouldn't know the man on the other side of the riverbank. Would you trust him to help you?

Trusting Levi Coffin

Many runaways were forced to trust people they did not know. You couldn't know everyone on the Underground Railroad. It was a very large and secret system. Still, some people with the railroad became quite well known. One such man was Levi Coffin.

Levi Coffin grew up in the South but hated slavery. He had been brought up as a Quaker. Quakers were against both slavery and violence.

As Coffin grew older, he wanted to change things. In 1826, he and his wife moved to Indiana, where he became a merchant. But his most important work was being an agent with the Underground Railroad.

The 1891 painting on this envelope shows Levi and Catherine Coffin helping fugitive slaves to safety. Painted by Charles Webber, a friend of the Coffins, it shows the Underground Railroad and the work of abolitionists. Catharine Coffin is standing in the center with the elderly gentleman using a walking stick, and her husband Levi Coffin is up high on the cart at the right.

Levi Coffin, shown with his wife, Catherine, also opened a store selling goods made by freed slaves.

For over twenty years Coffin turned his eight-room home into an Underground Railroad station. It became known as a safe place for runaways. Passengers on many different Underground Railroad routes used it.

Levi Coffin helped so many slaves that he became known as the president of the Underground Railroad. His house was later nicknamed Grand Central Station. That was the name of a very busy real railroad station in New York City.

Runaway slaves knew they could go there at any hour of the day or night. They'd tap on the window and Coffin would whisper for them to come in. Everyone spoke in hushed tones. No one ever knew who could be watching or listening outside.

Slave catchers often told people they were leaving. Then from a distance, they'd closely watch the house.

Later on, the Coffin family moved to Ohio. Levi still remained active on the Underground Railroad. In 1854, Coffin went to Canada for a meeting. Hundreds of former slaves came out to thank him. Coffin had sheltered and fed many of these people as far back as twenty years earlier.

What Would YOU Do?

❀ Would you work as an agent for the Underground Railroad? *Or . . .*

❀ Would you take an even more dangerous job? Would you be a conductor? You'd be leading slaves on a very daring path to freedom.

A Conductor on the Underground Railroad

Many people worked as conductors on the Underground Railroad. Being a conductor was especially dangerous. Conductors often led slaves directly out of the South. They did so in many ways. Sometimes they went on foot. Other times they drove wagons with hidden bottoms. The runaways were hidden there. Some conductors were even ship captains. They hid runaway slaves on their boats.

Fugitive slave Harriet Tubman was nicknamed Moses, like the biblical hero who led his people to freedom.

Among the best known Underground Railroad conductors was an escaped slave named Harriet Tubman. Tubman was a small woman who was born a slave in Maryland in about 1820. Her life was filled with hard work and painful beatings.

Tubman longed to be free. When she was about twenty-five, she ran away. She started out with two of her brothers. Her brothers became fearful and went back but Tubman went on alone. During the day, she hid in wooded areas. At night she traveled

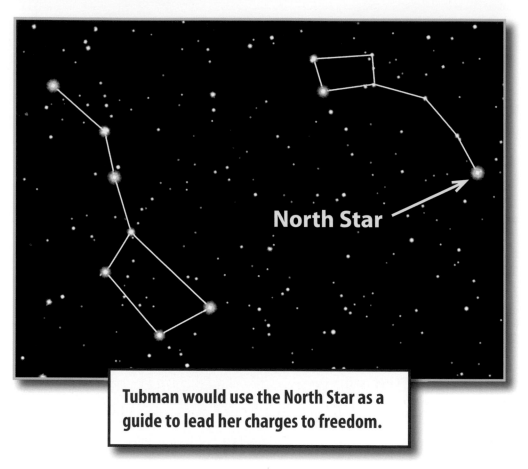

North Star

Tubman would use the North Star as a
guide to lead her charges to freedom.

by the light of the North Star. Runaways followed
the North Star to keep on course to the North. Soon
Tubman reached freedom.

Tubman began working as a conductor with the
Underground Railroad. Over ten years, she returned
to the South nineteen times. Going North wasn't easy.
Sometimes, Tubman's passengers wanted to turn back

but she wouldn't let them. She'd pull out a pistol and give them a choice. They'd go on or die!

Harriet Tubman led more than 300 slaves to freedom on the Underground Railroad. She could have been killed if caught. Yet she kept on and never lost a passenger!

What Would YOU Do?

❋ **Would you be a conductor on the Underground Railroad?** *Or . . .*

❋ **Would you pick a less dangerous way to help? You could show the passengers how to live successfully as free people. That was part of what the Underground Railroad also did.**

All They Needed

The Underground Railroad did much more than just bring runaways North. It also had a number of groups set up to help the former slaves find a place to live. The groups found jobs for them too.

Frederick Douglass was a famous runaway helped by a New York committee. Douglass soon became active with the Underground Railroad himself. He also became a well-known anti-slavery speaker and writer. His powerful words moved the hearts and minds of many people.

You didn't have to work on the Underground Railroad to help the system. One such man was a newspaper publisher named Elijah Lovejoy. Lovejoy often

Frederick Douglass was the leading black abolitionist in the country. He was a former slave who had run away to the North.

wrote articles against slavery and about the Underground Railroad. Slave owners wanted to put Lovejoy out of business. Pro-slavery mobs threw his printing presses into the Mississippi River three times.

On November 7, 1837, Lovejoy's fourth printing press arrived. Local slave owners found out about it. They demanded that he hand it over to them. Lovejoy would not do it. So a group of thugs attacked his warehouse. Shots rang out. Lovejoy was hit and died on the spot. The mob still destroyed the dead man's printing press. Then they threw the pieces into the Mississippi River.

Elijah P. Lovejoy

A mob gathered outside the offices of the *Alton Observer,* Elijah Lovejoy's newspaper. The mob set fire to the building and shot and killed Lovejoy.

What Would YOU Do?

❁ **Would you, like Elijah Lovejoy, risk your life to support the Underground Railroad?** *Or . . .*

❁ **Would you not want to take that risk? However, would you be willing to face the law and do prison time for your work on the Underground Railroad?**

When Things Went Wrong

Things did not always go well for Underground Railroad workers and passengers. Sometimes Underground Railroad plots were discovered. The runaways were returned to their owners. The Underground Railroad workers were often left to face the law.

That happened to ship Captain Daniel Drayton in 1847. He and another ship captain had planned a large-scale slave escape by water. They were going to take seventy-six slaves from Washington, D.C., to freedom.

Sadly, some slave owners found out about it. An armed police steamer overtook Drayton's ship.

Daniel Drayton was the captain of the *Pearl*, a boat on which seventy-seven slaves attempted to flee Washington, D.C., in April 1848. He was tried and eventually convicted for assisting in their escape.

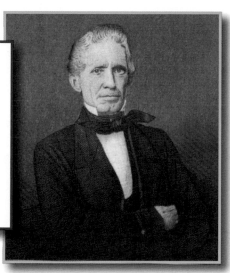

Slaves wearing handcuffs and shackles passing the United States Capitol, around 1815. Slaves and slave auctions were part of daily life in Washington, D.C.

Slaves were put on public display at auctions, while slave buyers shouted out bids. It was an humiliating experience that often ended in the slave being separated from his or her family.

He and the other ship captain were each fined $10,000. The men also went to prison for a time. The same thing sometimes happened to other Underground Railroad workers in slave escapes as well.

What Would YOU Do?

❋ Would you be willing to pay the legal price for your actions on the Underground Railroad? *Or . . .*

❋ Would you limit your activities for the Underground Railroad to just speaking out for the system?

Standing Behind the Underground Railroad

Sometimes, whole towns spoke out and protected the Underground Railroad.

This once happened in Attica, New York. Two slave catchers arrived in town. They were there for a runaway slave named Statie and her daughter.

The slave catchers asked the postmaster where the slaves were. The postmaster told them that the runaways were in town. They had been brought there by the Underground Railroad. He also said that if they tried to take the pair, every man, woman, and child would act to stop them. The postmaster warned the slave catchers to leave as soon as possible. He didn't think they'd be safe for much longer than about twenty minutes in town.

Whenever a slave escaped, the slave catchers were often close behind.

THREE HUNDRED DOLLARS REWARD.

RANAWAY from the subscriber on Monday the 17th ult., three negroes, named as follows: HARRY, aged about 19 years, has on one side of his neck a wen, just under the ear, he is of a dark chestnut color, about feet 8 or 9 inches hight; BEN, aged aged about 25 years, is very quick to speak when spoken to, he is of a chestnut color, about six feet high; MINTY, aged about 27 years, is of a chestnut color, fine looking, and about 5 feet high. One hundred dollars reward will be given for each of the above named negroes, if taken out of the State, and $50 each if taken in the State. They must be lodged in Baltimore, Easton or Cambridge Jail, in Maryland.

                              ELIZA ANN BRODESS.
        Near Bucktown, Dorchester county, Md
Oct. 3d, 1849.

Wanted posters offering rewards were often posted to entice people to turn in runaway slaves. This is a wanted poster for Harriet Tubman who was known as Minty at the time.

The slave catchers quickly saw the truth. A large crowd was already gathering in the street. Some had weapons. Others were shouting for the slave catchers to leave. The slave catchers mounted their horses and speedily rode out of town. As they rode off the crowd loudly cheered.

What Would YOU Do?

❀ **Would you have come out to stand up to the slave catchers?** *Or . . .*

❀ **Would you have stayed safely at home?**

An Important Reminder

Over the years, many people helped with the Underground Railroad. It was an important path to freedom for slaves. Yet it was also much more.

The Underground Railroad was what the United States badly needed during a difficult time. It was a great symbol of freedom. People from different backgrounds worked together to make it succeed. It showed that with courage and hard work important changes could be made.

In the end, the Underground Railroad quietly faded away. When the North won the Civil War

Levi Coffin and Catherine Coffin

Frederick Douglass

Daniel Drayton

Elijah Lovejoy

Harriet Tubman

All these people made a life or death decision. What would you do?

in 1865, slavery was banned. There was no longer a need for an Underground Railroad.

Yet the memory of the Underground Railroad remains. It's an important reminder for the nation. It shows us that goodness can exist even in the darkest times.

Timeline

1600s to mid-1800s—Slavery is legal in some parts of the United States.

1793—The Fugitive Slave Act of 1793 is passed. This act makes it illegal to help runaway slaves.

1820—At about this year, Harriet Tubman is born. She becomes one of the best known Underground Railroad conductors.

1826—Levi Coffin and his wife move to Indiana. They become very active on the Underground Railroad at this time. Levi Coffin later becomes known as the president of the Underground Railroad.

1837—Elijah Lovejoy's fourth printing press arrives. It triggers a mob attack in which Lovejoy is killed.

1847—Ship Captain Daniel Drayton begins a large-scale slave escape that fails.

1850—The Fugitive Slave Act of 1850 is passed. It strengthens the earlier Fugitive Slave Act.

1854—Levi Coffin goes to Canada for a meeting. Hundreds of former Underground Railroad passengers come out to greet and thank him.

1865—The North wins the Civil War. Slavery is banned, ending the need for an Underground Railroad.

Words to Know

abolitionist—A person who believed that slavery should be outlawed.

congressman—A person elected to represent a group of people in government.

The Fugitive Slave Acts—Acts that made it against the law to help runaway slaves.

ice floes—Pieces of ice that have broken away from a frozen lake or river.

mob—A rough and violent group of people.

network—A group of people who are connected or work with one another in some way.

route—A system of roads to be followed to get from one place to another.

steamer—A boat powered by steam.

symbol—Something that stands for something else.

torture—Brutal treatment meant to cause extreme pain.

Learn More

Books

Fradin, Dennis Brindell. *The Underground Railroad*. Tarrytown, N.Y.: Benchmark Books, 2009.

Haskins, Jim, ed. *Black Stars of Civil War Times*. Hoboken, N.J.: John Wiley and Sons, 2003.

McPherson, James M. *Fields of Fury: The American Civil War*. New York: Atheneum Books for Young Readers, 2002.

Petry, Ann. *Harriet Tubman: Conductor on the Underground Railroad*. Logan, IA.: Perfection Learning, 2001.

Stanchak, John. *Civil War*. New York: Dorling Kindersley Publishers Ltd., 2001.

Williams, Carla. *The Underground Railroad*. Mankato, Minn.: Child's World, 2009.

Web Sites

National Geographic Education: The Underground Railroad
<http://education.nationalgeographic.com/education/multimedia/interactive/the-underground-railroad/?ar_a=1>

National Underground Railroad Freedom Center
<http://www.freedomcenter.org>

Index